WHY DO I
DRIBBLE?

BY HARRIET BRUNDLE

BookLife
PUBLISHING

©2018
BookLife Publishing
King's Lynn
Norfolk PE30 4LS

All rights reserved.
Printed in Malaysia.

A catalogue record for this
book is available from the
British Library.

ISBN: 978-1-78637-365-6

Written by:
Harriet Brundle

Edited by:
Kirsty Holmes

Designed by:
Danielle Rippengill

Image Credits

All images are courtesy of Shutterstock.com, unless otherwise specified. With thanks to Getty Images, Thinkstock Photo and iStockphoto. Front Cover & 1 – Dmitry Natashin, Nadzin, Sudowoodo, Sunflowerr. Images used on every spread – Nadzin, TheFarAwayKingdom. 2 – svtdesign, vectorplus, anpannan. 4 – Iconic Bestiary. 5 – Makc, Iconic Bestiary. 6 – Iconic Bestiary. 7 – Le_Mon, Ienjoyeverytime. 8 – LOVE YOU. 9 – MaryValery. 10 & 11 – Le_Mon, Iconic Bestiary. 12 – Iconic Bestiary, Maxim Cherednichenko, Sudowoodo. 13 – Iconic Bestiary. 14 – world of vector, Ign. 15 – Iconic Bestiary, Karolina Madej, VikiVector. 16 – Le_Mon, wissanustock, Ienjoyeverytime. 17 – svtdesign, vectorplus, anpannan. 18 & 19 – Le_Mon. 20 – Meranda19. 21 – Pretty Vectors, Skokan Olena. 22 – Iconic Bestiary, Miuky. 23 – Ign, ArtMaster85, Artem Twin, George J.

CONTENTS

Words that look like **this** can be found in the glossary on page 24.

Is Your mouth Watering?

When you've got something tasty for dinner, does your mouth water at the thought?

Think about your favourite food. Is your mouth starting to water?

Have you ever woken up to find you have dribbled on your pillow?

Our bodies make loads of dribble every day. The question is, what is it and why do we do it?

Crunch and Slurp

When we eat, we use our teeth to chew our food into smaller pieces. This makes the food easier for our bodies to **digest**.

When we chew our food, our mouths make lots of dribble, or saliva. This saliva helps us to start digesting the food we are eating before we swallow it.

Saliva is mostly made of water. It also contains enzymes which help break down food.

Mega mouths

Inside our mouths there are different body parts which form part of our digestive **system**, helping us to digest our food.

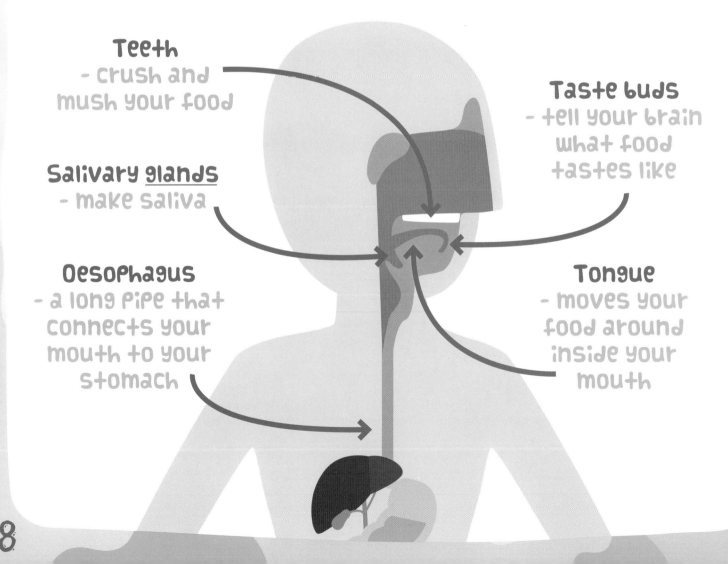

Teeth
- crush and mush your food

Salivary glands
- make saliva

Oesophagus
- a long pipe that connects your mouth to your stomach

Taste buds
- tell your brain what food tastes like

Tongue
- moves your food around inside your mouth

Saliva also helps to keep our mouths **moist**.

Imagine trying to talk or swallow without any saliva. It would be almost impossible!

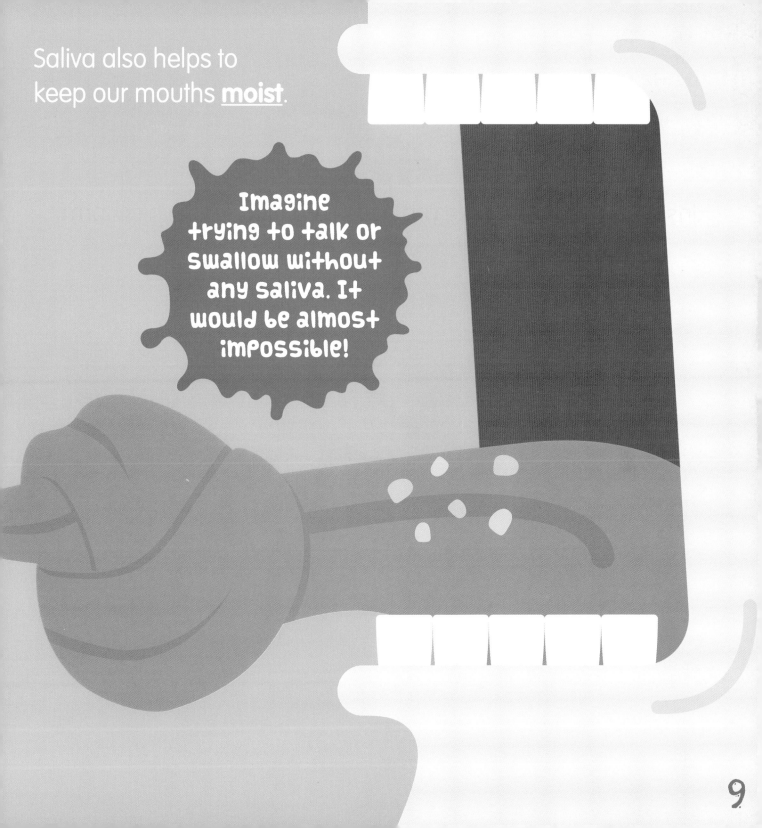

Chew and Swallow

STEP 1:

As soon as you take a bite of food, your saliva is go, go, GO!

STEP 2:

As your teeth begin to chomp down on the food, your salivary glands release saliva into your mouth. The more you chomp, the more saliva is released.

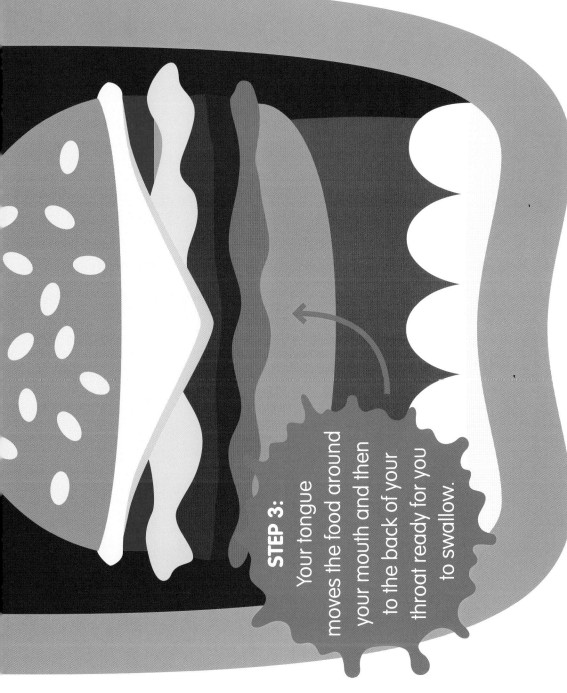

STEP 3: Your tongue moves the food around your mouth and then to the back of your throat ready for you to swallow.

STEP 4: The ball of food slips down your throat in a stream of saliva.

11

Dribble Dribble

Has your mouth ever watered when you've smelt some delicious food?

When your brain thinks you're about to eat, it fires up your salivary glands. They prepare your mouth for the meal you're about to have by filling it with saliva!

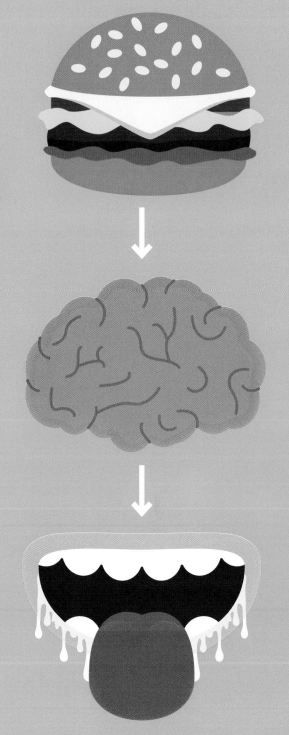

While we are awake, we swallow our saliva. At night time, we're not awake to swallow it, so the dribble can leak out of your mouth and onto your pillow!

Stick Your Tongue Out

Don't forget to brush your tongue when you brush your teeth. This helps to keep it clean and give you fresh breath!

Our tongues are covered in taste buds. Each person has thousands of taste buds on their tongue.

Our taste buds tell our brain what food tastes like. Our tongues can taste salty, sweet, sour, bitter and **umami**.

Some people love the taste of bitter lemons while others love super-sweet ice cream!

Show Us Your Teeth

We have different types of teeth which work together to munch and crunch our food.

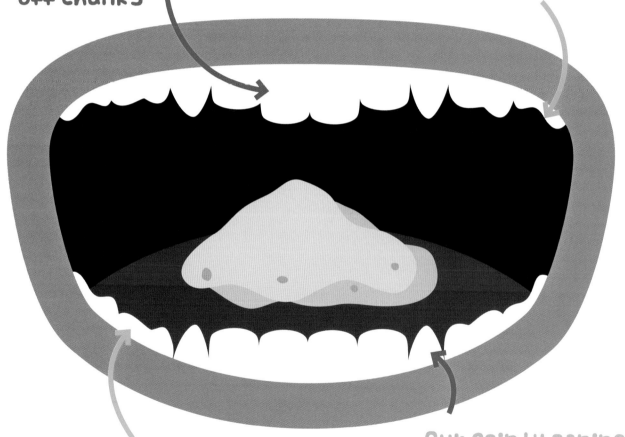

Our incisors **bite off chunks**

Our molars **are our biggest teeth and they chew and grind**

Our pre-molars **have a flatter surface to crush**

Our pointy canines **rip and tear**

Superhero Saliva!

Even though our teeth are covered in seriously strong **enamel**, our saliva helps out to look after our teeth.

Saliva around our teeth helps to fight off **bacteria** which can cause **tooth decay**.

A Recipe for Dribble

Our dribble is made up of a special mix of different ingredients…

Around 99% of our saliva is made of water.

Enzymes help to start breaking down the food we eat before we swallow it.

Saliva helps to keep our mouth moist so we can speak and swallow.

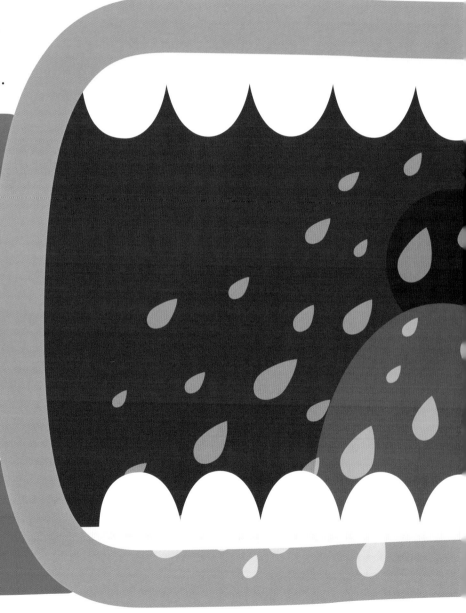

Some <u>hormones</u> are present in our saliva.

Our saliva works every day to help keep our mouths clean and healthy.

Bits of food stuck between our teeth can be washed away by saliva.

Anything else we put in our mouths, like toothpaste, can be found in our saliva.

Dust or dirt can end up in our mouths too!

19

Super Spit!

Did you know that dribble has several different super powers?

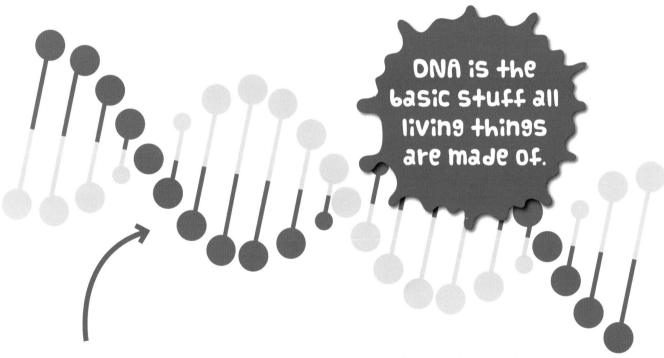

ONA is the basic stuff all living things are made of.

Information about our bodies can be found inside our mouths. When a simple swab of your cheek is tested, it can reveal **DNA** information about you!

In our spit there is a substance called opiorphin, which is an extremely strong painkiller!

Vampire bat saliva could help to treat strokes. Strokes can be caused by a blood clot and vampire bat spit contains an enzyme which stops blood from clotting.

Dribble Trivia

Saliva helps cuts in your mouth heal faster than a cut anywhere else on your body!

Each year you produce enough dribble to fill two bath tubs!

Just like in our kidneys, our salivary glands can develop stones.

The longest stone ever removed from a human body was 37mm and weighed 3.597G.

Brian Krause holds the record of 28.51m for the longest spit of a cherry stone in a competition!

When you're feeling nervous or frightened, you might find that you produce less saliva. This gives the feeling of having a dry mouth.

Glossary

bacteria	small living organisms that can cause infection
decay	rot as a result of bacteria
digest	break down food
DNA	responsible for the features each person has
enamel	a hard substance which is a protective coating for our teeth
enzymes	a substance which causes a specific reaction
glands	an organ which produces a substance
hormones	chemicals which make our cells and organs do things
moist	damp or wet
system	a set of things working together to do a job
umami	a savoury taste

Index